REALM OF THE POSSIBLE

Also by Sharon Dolin:

Heart Work
Serious Pink

Chapbooks:
Climbing Mount Sinai
Mind Lag
Mistakes
The Seagull

REALM OF THE POSSIBLE

Sharon Dolin

Four Way Books
New York City

Distributed by
University Press of
New England
Hanover and
London

Editorial Office
Four Way Books
POB 535, Village Station
New York, NY 10014
www.fourwaybooks.com

Library of Congress Catalogue Card Number: 2002116859

ISBN 1-884800-57-2

Cover art: *Goldfish in Pond* by J. Somers
By permission of the collector

This book is manufactured in the United States of America
and printed on acid-free paper.

Four Way Books is a division of Friends of Writers, Inc., a Vermont-based not-for-profit organization. We are grateful for the assistance we receive from individual donors and private foundations.

Distributed by University Press of New England
One Court Street, Lebanon, NH 03766

ACKNOWLEDGMENTS

Grateful acknowledgment is made to the following publications where the following poems appeared, some in earlier versions:

The Alembic: "Japanese Beetles"

The American Voice: "The Naturalist Declares Her Ignorance," "Stroke"

The Amicus Journal: "My Soul's Wardrobe"

Barrow Street: "Realm of the Possible"

Boulevard: "The Problem of Desertion"

Connecticut Review: "Past the Allowable Limit of Grief," "Osgood Pond"

Faultline: "Olivetta"

5 AM: "Betrayal," "Hands"

Judaism: "Spring Rites"

The Kenyon Review: "Life Is Not What You"

Kerem: "Believers in Mercy"

Literary Imagination: "Roman Punch"

Pequod: "The Dance"

Ploughshares: "Uncanny"

Poetry International: "Krupp's Walk"

Response: "Mortal Love"

RUNES: "The Seagull," "On Reading Amichai's *Open Closed Open* While Suckling Samuel"

St. Luke's Review: "Aubade," "Verona at Dusk"

Salamander: "Firenze Dream," "Summer's Pitcher"

Sugar Mule: "Final Labor"

The Threepenny Review: "Blue Dutch Tin"

Tin House: "Berzerkly," "Eyed"

"The Seagull" was published as a limited-edition letterpress chapbook, *The Seagull* (The Center for Book Arts, 2001).

"My Soul's Wardrobe" appeared in the anthology *Poetry Comes Up Where It Can: Poems from* The Amicus Journal, *1990-2000* (The University of Utah Press, 2000), edited by Brian Swann, with an introduction by Mary Oliver.

"Opening the Scroll," "Climbing Mount Sinai," "Mortal Love," "Rain," "Geniza," "On the Unmiraculous," and "The Believers in Mercy" were published in the letterpress chapbook, *Climbing Mount Sinai* (Dim Gray Bar Press, 1996).

"The Apology" appeared in the pamphlet, *Sarajevo: Witnesses of Existence* (1994), in conjunction with a benefit exhibition at the New York Kuntshalle for the Open Stage Obala Theatre in Sarajevo.

Thanks to *www.PoetryMagazine.com* for republishing online "The Seagull" and "Realm of the Possible."

With gratitude to Phillis Levin, Rachel Wetzsteon, Jeff Friedman, and Chana Bloch for their incisive comments on the poems in this book. Special thanks to Martha Rhodes for her close reading. I am grateful to Ellen Geist, Rachel Weintraub, Jeanne Marie Beaumont, Peter Covino, Gardner McFall, Patricia Carlin, Alfredo Rossi, and Yerra Sugarman for their support and encouragement in this writing life. Finally, I wish to thank the Corporation of Yaddo and the Virginia Center for the Creative Arts, where some of these poems were written and revised.

This publication is made possible with a regrant from the Council of Literary Magazines and Presses, supported by public funds from the New York State Council on the Arts, a state agency.

For Barry and Sam,
who continue to show me what is possible

CONTENTS

III

IV

My soul, do not seek immortal life,
but exhaust the realm of the possible.

—Pindar, *Pythian Odes, III*

LIFE IS NOT WHAT YOU

expected—cows
ruminate by the highway
even in rain or bat their
ears forward and back and how
you thought the story of your life
would get told: the children you thought
you'd already have by now partially grown
books and other accomplishments—houses
owned cities seen lakes traversed—and now
we're stuck in traffic
and it's not even rush hour
with the hurricane storm
moving slowly north from Alabama.
How come it's raining here already
somewhere south of Albany—just one
damned thing after another and those
injections you've had to give yourself and
your dad's bypass surgery. Just look:
     Evening primrose all along the roadside match
     the painted line and Queen Anne's lace
             on the other side rows of young corn
             joe-pye weed blurred to Scottish heather.
When you go for a walk blackberries have started
    ripening you   pluck two
from each bush notice tadpoles suck air
    along the fountain's rim. Such small swishings
of joy maybe
             this is it—every day puts forth a new song deer flies
             dive-bombing your head when the breeze
             lets up—

3

JAPANESE BEETLES

It all comes down to killing and feasting
            or coupling, doesn't it.
Strolled the great sloping
                lawn to the fountain—stopped by a clustered iridescence
turning in the grass—kneeled—as it kept turning and growing
                catching the sun in golds purples lustrous
metal-greens. Imbricate—like the scales of a pine cone continuously
                recomposing itself—all turned

around a core of two it seemed
they must be coupling—and the others
                all latched on in aid supportive bustling or could it be vicarious
pleasure—as did I with a grass blade barely able to coax
one away before he wandered back as though to a brilliant
                            spinning magnet. So I rose and walked off
through the woods where white slips of moths darted

            in the mud and mosquitoes made lunch of my exposed
back despite White Flower Balm from Hong Kong. This churning
hive has stayed with me even if soon they will fly
to eat the nearby roses and lay their larvae

in the leaves. This morning a wasp
with its iridescent blue belly
    has died—one brown wing extended—on my floor and so instead of being
something else's breakfast she is mine—at least to admire
her shining thorax and ovipositor-sting.
I scoop her up for a paper burial. I don't know
                what to do in this world but play

the notes of these letters off against whatever it is I've seen. Call it
a kind of
coupling of thing with thing: buzz of cicada or firefly
            flash with scratch of black letters. In the woods a composer
makes his own mockingbird notes—mine are borrowed from the wind.

UNCANNY

When the beekeeper
who lived in a cabin—perched
on the side of a mountain—also
a sketcher of rocks boulders
and lone trees beaten sideways by wind
was visited one night
by the shepherd who lived in the valley
he served him dinner the way Abraham hurried
to greet the hungry angel
when the shepherd reached to pay for so much
wine and conversation skillet potatoes with bacon
the beekeeper pushed the money back
and cursed
You're spitting on my pleasure
the shepherd froze
backed up stiffly
holding an unlit cigarette
tears rolled down his
cheeks then down
the other's in such stillness
both stood until they slowly raised
their arms and embraced.

At which point I looked up
with moist eyes
from my subway seat to find
a tall black man neatly dressed
in a new leather jacket and gloves
but with something wrong
with his face huge tears
coursed down both
cheeks behind his sunglasses
it being fluorescent night
he removed to slowly wipe his face
then replace but the tears

8

kept coming on and he
had to continually remove
his glasses and wipe
his face all done
with no sound and I wanted
to—white and a woman
and in New York—
stand and embrace him.

REALM OF THE POSSIBLE

Now that he had reached the age of forty, he would never become
a pianist or learn Japanese, he was sure of it. . . . Perhaps all things
had been possible but they were no longer. —Cees Nooteboom

We climb to Villa Jovis
in a sweat
no longer in our first marriages
but thriving into this present
that sweeps us up to gape
closed-mouthed at the sea, at rocks jutting up,
dotted with cypresses and pines.

We've come to the summit
to poke among bricks and imagine
an aging emperor carried uphill
past olive trees and pomegranates, lemons
and tomatoes, sprays of agave and oleander
so he might watch the room-sized cisterns being refilled
before he soaked in a sea-water bath.

Maybe all things are no longer possible
yet late, past forty, you learned Greek
well enough to read yesterday of the origin
of men and women—those four-footed, four-handed,
two-headed beasts, split apart so love could become
the name for the desire and pursuit of the whole.

At forty, I can say at least I am
a cognoscente of the sea:
knowing how to immerse myself
without regrets or direction
letting the currents trundle me
to a cove where small black fish sway
and then dip while feeding.

Today I finally swam into the grotto
with its vaulted ceiling, blue midnight
waters and echoing slap, all the while
companioned by my fear.

Now on a hillside in the dusk
as the sea lifts and pastels into sky
and the crickets' percussive buzz
is a twilight song of self

I wonder what is still possible
when you dub me your "current wife,"
meaning only to place us in the midst
of the momentary.

I'm going to slip these words into the current
among orange-striped powder-blue fish
down into an underwater cove
like Salvia, who dug up a jug of Tiberius's
wine, mixed it into his barrels
so all his wine would be related.

So my being late in finding you
and enjoying where I am
I wed and toss to these waters, these ancient
cicadas, these rocks waist deep in the sea.

BETRAYAL

It's true we're all betrayers and without question
    the truth shimmers behind and through and in
    the veil.

The woman—aunt(?) of a boisterous five-year-old
    kicking me slightly, unable to calm down and nap—
    returning from holiday in Napoli,

Offers a biscuit, accepts a question: The boy,
    Bosnian, for forty days has sojourned in the embraces
    of this Red Cross mother

Adopting mother with mother tongue and wearing
    his cross on the outside, asks to peek
    and see where hers is hidden.

Who now transports him back over the border
    to an orphanage. (*He doesn't even have a dog for relation.*)
    Who, to calm him, after a sleepless night

Threatens to send him off with the conductor:
    Andrea, sei cattivo! winking at me and the conductor
    who plays along, motioning to him

To behave or else. And the boy believes and disbelieves,
    caught between stations: between having a name and having
    a hand grownups take and say, *Come with me.*

BERZERKLY

Friends. Lovers. Colleagues. What
would you call us that fall
    so far back it belongs to another age

when ambition barely kept pace
with a desperate will to couple?
    I entered yours through a cookbook; we

three made dinner—or you did—vegetarian quiche
spiced up with talk of *jouissance* &
    the lack. My skin

was all that showed shoved up against
your perfect French & films foreign from
    further back. Berkeley then one huge tongue

lapping cappuccino froth, fruit smoothies, nipples.
Lacking *jouissance* I became your step-
    child confidante turned courtesan

reclining on the couch, listening to Miles
& reading *Pleasures of the Text* until late
    I'd cycle—or he'd drive me—back.

How did the night of pearls happen—round your neck
teeth down your blouse being unbuttoned? Was I
    still dressed? I only remember the two of you

wanted me there—why—to watch
or fondle not to share him he
    was yours your body said slipping

under him why did I stay—hungry
hoping to be next when you pulled all
    the strings of this ménage

out of my reach until one weekend you left us
to playact at dating. Over dinner he spilled
    he'd helped build a nuclear power

plant, this budding Socialist, for a higher
summer wage. Back on your bed
    I gulped him like plonk & choked. Why

bother stealing still I knew you'd be enraged;
our necklace broke, we never spoke again.
    Were you testing me was I testing you to see

how far you'd give? Payback for the night
you made me watch and grabbed my hands
    to fondle you. I did—or did I—almost

forget about you until last night
your face on TV after a score
    of years: the same gap-toothed smile same

silky-hair string of pearls now Manet's Olympia
staring down at you from her divan
    buck naked dropped in naughty demotic.

The hearsay bobbing up: You were known
for placing ads *Single Woman Wanted by Couple*.
    Not learning till later I fit a part, I unhooked

myself from you like leaving a cult.
The first man I met in an outdoor café
    took me home to show me Rorschach

blots. What did I see? No kidding.
Were we all crazed back then
    or what?

ROMAN PUNCH

Looking up we see the same light tolling
upon the same shuttered windows and the same
dark high-heeled swagger serve us coffee
like an affront, like the heat that smacks us
in the face as we climb the Gianicolo for a view

of Pulchinello hitting his rival with a stick
as the children squeal until Death comes
to ask for a dance saying, *Look me in the eyes*
to the sweating horde who lean against parked
cars exhaling music through their doors.

Someone has hung a pair of jeans out the window
onto the piazza so the shutters form its windy torso.

But is it poetry when the slick mud of a pigeon
blisters my eye and page? *Porta fortuna,*
the dark-haired one sighed. *Maybe you will
go away,* breathed her friend.

As though luck could be flung down like an espresso
or we could be made to leave this soon.

EYED

In Napoli, as everyone expected,
    I was—at Mergellina station—
eyed and flirted

with, by a five-foot barman
    who drank me up as I sipped
lemon soda and prated on

about New York, then sped
    down to where he said I'd find
a toilet. His words led

to an empty café, a tall boy mind-
    ing the bar, on his face the fuzz
of a first beard. He gestured behind

the counter, I was
    somewhat disarmed,
followed him gingerly—yet it does

make me wonder even now, though unharmed,
    why he didn't charge
me 200 lire (I bought nothing). What small alarm

went off inside as he seemed to barge
    in a hurry into another
room suddenly, I had an urge—

how can I say, whatever
    thickens the air
in August, it was uneasy weather—

to beware;
    before I'd unbutton,
poked, examined, sniffed everywhere

16

perused again in slow motion
        (stray mops were flung, water
in a pail) as though I were driven

before I'd drop a romper
        dress that would
have bared me in bra

—stubbornly still dressed, I stood
        not usually so exercised
in paranoia, studied the wood

walls a long minute until I spied
        a keyhole
to which I put my eye:

Close as a fish just float-
        ing in its
viscous wet bloat

swam a dark something
        I'd never seen before:
Call it pure looking;

it might have been a mirror
        a body become
nothing but viewer

not a transparency (I grew numb)
        but an all-bodied
intensity that beat (for a stunned

second) there lidless, until my voice
        screamed itself a shutter
Non voglio! (Fear left no choice.)

So I fled: How many others
        on their way to Pompeii, chic resorts
on Capri that summer

hiked up their skirts
        slipped panties down in total
ease or need, or else yanked down their shorts?

The tanned Scandinavians, frugal
        Germans, eager Americans
may have—or were some skeptical

like me? Why wonder if I was the only woman
        —his speed means
he was practiced at being hidden.

Maybe my scream is what he retains
        from that summer—as his eye
swimming in its keyholed lair remains

my only sight of Napoli.
        Didn't he later
go up and lie

about my hidden charms to the shorter
        barman after I ran upstairs
to tell my husband of my latest scrape with danger?

FILENE'S BASEMENT

Dizzily trying on dresses then returning
    to scan the racks out of anxious tedium in need

of comfort I spied a man eyeing the racks
    from the side cautiously at first as if he were

an embarrassed husband in lingerie then more boldly
    pulling out first one dress then another and holding it

up to model slyly refraining from glancing around I
    malingered to watch half out of curiosity half pity

how far would he allow himself to go did he see me
    watching was his dejection any greater than mine

gone to hunt for solace among racks of ill-fitting
    gowns finally I slunk away having reached

bottom where the scale was balanced between self-pity /
    sorrow over being his mirror.

THE DANCE

Stopped short at Times
Square in early rush
hour from barreling

along my usual
diagonal in the sub-
terranean hall between

one train and my
connection. A crowd had
gathered in a loose

semicircle around
a dancing couple:
A man in a forties fedora,

a dark moustache,
was leading a spangled beauty
with accentuated moves

as though she might not follow:
First he dipped her
to the floor then stood

her up again—
his arm across her back
shook until her backside

ruffle jiggled.
The crowd clapped.
Her long hair

was raven
black and snaky,
a bit too shiny. He kept

her back to us
to enhance the spell. *Oye,*
todo el mundo . . .

was all I caught
of the Latin ballad, her skin—
bone-white, silver sequins

hugged her torso.
All the while I
kept angling

for the pathway
to my train, yet
I had to stay

until I caught her face
—a face that had
todo el mundo

(or at least this
circle) transfixed.
In the white-tiled passageway,

where all routes meet
and cross, hadn't they found
the perfect woman

who bowed and swung to life
where he pushed her:
one of those dolls

whose puckered mouth
is ruled
by a kiss.

Even after the show
when he takes her home,
empties all the change

out of his hat
(Can your mind not stray
to it?) *Mira,*

sometimes doesn't he
lay down with her—no
backtalk

his pleasure, their
dancing since they
both move together?

Todo el mundo (Come to
think of it, they were
all men) gaping with envy

at the dancer
ventriloquizing
her body (so it felt

how—) I backed
away (pornographic)
refused to become

some mute thing
in the face of
someone's cravings.

Another rush hour,
the glistening eyes
of the mesmerized crowd

say the couple's back:
    Now she's a blonde in red,
he's swinging her pliant

      limbs to life.
    Why stop? And yet—
wasn't I once

      bereft enough
    to partner with the dead
(circle right, circle left)—

      why
hurry by?

FORMS OF MASTERY

Say "I hate me" and I'll throw you the ball
and his younger brother does
in a parroted tongue so each gets what he wants.
In this way the boys play at mastery
against the sweetened backdrop of a lake
called childhood.

In this way the pines absorb the shouts
along with birdcalls and the wind
braids light and shadow all across the lake's span
then does to the lake what time does to us: wrinkles
then flattens the parchment till it's smooth.

Three years ago I paddled with a tense soul
off the shores of Monterosso.
Evening he offered me a troubled piece of light
set in gold and I said yes to a different kind
of mastery: to desire that singed the giver
and the given until in less than a month
he was undone by what he could not overcome.

Nearly two years ago
the one you'd wed
crashed from the sky.
For a year you tended your grief
at the world's randomness
then brought her ashes to the lake.

Now our separate losses have been braided
into an almost invisible sheen—

the pale blue surface of the lake
called our life together.

Early morning or late afternoon
when the edges scissor themselves into jagged
pieces that roughen the surface,
we take out the canoe, glide slowly over it together.

AMBER

He discovered them while moving the antique dresser,
pulling out all the drawers;
        they slipped onto the floor.
Why leave them out—if not for you to wear?

You hold the strung beads up: real or plastic?
Irregular cubes of marmalade-mottled
        translucence. Guess they're fossil
resin, from somewhere along the Baltic.

You peer within: no insects buried.
They were his late wife's—hidden
        for at least seven
years where once they'd slid.

Now unentombed, revisited
by light and a woman's
        hands. You slip them on,
then off, admiring them, strung and knotted

along a copper thread, and finger their dull luster.
What makes you begin to count?
        Think you'll figure out
they were her prized worry beads?

You can tell, before finishing, there are forty
—exactly her age
        when she burned up in the fuselage.
Inhabiting what once was hers: Does he think it's easy?

In your study her bookshelves house your books;
in the corner her handmade table snugly fits.
        Is it all right to wear these beads
as once or twice you've worn her pearls?

If you do, what might happen?
Wash off the dust.
        Counter it:
In the face of fear and repulsion

imagine if suddenly *you* were gone.
Would you really mind your bracelet of honeyed amber,
        silver-rimmed, flecked by insects and fire,
adorning the wrist of another woman?

Picture *her,* in turn,
like you, musing over
        what to preserve,
what can still be worn.

VERONA AT DUSK

On the hill beyond
      cypresses are first
to speak of night

while the Lamberti Tower
      rotates
its minutes and hours,

terracotta roofs, striped
      stone and ochre brick,
and rose cobbles pulse with light.

The wingèd lion poised with a book
      at one end of Piazza delle Erbe:
What could he be reading

while Madonna Verona, draped
      in stony folds
atop her fountain, loosely holds a banner?

La Vita Nuova of Dante, whose lady
      in a dream Love bade
consume his heart. See how he stands,

in the next piazza, two fingers on a cheek while
      musing over the twin secrets
of his art: early death of the beloved and exile.

But need it be the arc of every story?
      From this twilit window
where a rainbow sends pale flares against the night

I see the early deaths, our being drawn
      together so we may hold a different book
up to the honeyed light before we journey home.

THE PROBLEM OF DESERTION

occurs when time feels like space
and the dead are stuck
on shore
            while we
            the living kneeling in our form-
                        fitted canoes
                        paddle on the lake
                                    into years past trees
                                    whole rivers of lily pads and reeds

and all they do
            like the loon's echoing call on the farthest shore

is recede
recede.

II

GENIZA

in memory of Billy Gelfond (1957-1993)

SUMMER'S PITCHER

Now the Water Carrier is gone
nameless birds wake me
so I pour out the pitcher
of tears

watch the grass—
it opens
as though my gaze
were the worm of fertility:

Clover, crabgrass, daisies
part and fuse—

they are the fruit of where
he has gone

his pitcher having emptied itself
into the earth

mine I raise up
to the sun

        slowly refill
        with iridescent insect wings
        the buzz of summer
        cicadas, the velvet

        hush of a stand of
        trees through which
        his soul   has blown.

GENIZA

If geniza is where
the tattered bodies of books
ripped parchment
with the Holy Name
are entombed,

you must be there, with
your life broken in half
like the angry rod of Moses.

I hope you made it to the big one
in Cairo, city of lost chants,
forgotten corridors, smoky passageways,
strong hashish.

My heart
a geniza of broken loves:
the greatest one (you) flung
on top.

FINAL LABOR

On that day
silence
enthroned the world:

in between the laughter of friends,
a hollow hum.

For two years you held up the sky.

Robbed now of those golden apples

I return to where
the horizon has dropped
into me

as you—scorpion
caught in the ring
of fire—

stung yourself—
dropped
burning.

ON THE UNMIRACULOUS

When the Prophet Elisha
passed before the gate
of the Shunammite woman,
she gave him bread
and asked for nothing.

In time, she prepared a room
for his visits soon more frequent
going to and fro upon the earth:
a bed, a table, a candlestick,
a simple place in the attic.

When he asked what he could do for her,
she replied, *I need no one.*
I dwell among my own people.
Barren, old, unasked, she was told,
By this time next year you'll have a son.

So blessed, the couple lived their life.
Years passed, until her boy, running up
from the fields, clutching his head and crying,
My head, my head, then quickly dying.

Still at home in the miraculous,
the woman from Shunem laid him out on the Prophet's bed
then ran to summon Elisha from Mount Carmel
who rose, climbed down, and saw
in his attic room, the child laid
out on the bed—cold, stone dead.

He prayed before touching
the boy's head.
Then did what only God did:
laid himself upon the child
and breathed spirit into nostrils

and mouth—vigor
through the fingers of the hands
and the child, warmed,
sneezed seven times and
seized his soul back
into his body.

All this I repeat upon
the solitary air
having only the husks of story
to fill the winter
and no miracles to record
only the outer shell of prayer.

THE APOLOGY

You have gone
and hidden yourself

where, unlike Orpheus,
I cannot follow

and where these songs
may never reach.

You threw the dice
of your life hard

against the wall
of your heart

knocked your head
against

the mirror of self
and it broke you.

I apologize
for not going

down to retrieve you
having always

been one
who looks back.

MORTAL LOVE

The Nephilim were in the earth
in those days, and also after that,
when the sons of God came in
unto the daughters of men . . . .
           —Genesis VI, 4

All day long I lived canopied
by your beauty
held
over me: warm-blooded
giant, one of the Nephilim,
smitten
who wedded the daughters of women.

Descended from them—diminished
you hovered over
wings enfolded
in your back

when I embraced you
I rode
the mortal place we meet

pulling you
permanently
down from sky
to die   before we rose, firmly
planted on Earth.

RAIN

Now the rain bends the pines
and I pine for you a little
bit less. Was it only a year ago
you took me to the rose garden

Where we posed by the fountain
in shades, as though we might be recognized,
gazed up at the mansion
from whose stone steps I gaze down.

Went to see the trotters, tossed
bets and won back all we'd lost.

A month later, betrothed on a terrace
under the Mediterranean night,
we thought our names
would merge, yield other names.

Then the year turned. While we sat in a pew
the Angel of Death selected,
wrote you in the book that, gradually,
fills with all our names.

And though you fasted and prayed,
we didn't know the ink was drying,
the book closing, nearly sealed.
The Sabbath Angels came to cloak you

In your second soul—too late; with one stroke,
you tore the parchment of your life
I still scroll back and read
but to which you can no longer add.

THE SCAPEGOAT

Little, scrawny, with barely enough hair
on my forelegs to count for fur
I weather their wrath poured out
upon my back: this one's eclipsed

eye at the suicide, the guilty ones who stood by,
that one's poor mothering, another's fury
at my long teeth and vigorous lips plucking the weeds,
munching on anything that might be useful.

I shoulder them all on my lumbering ribs.
My globular eyes
could have been a fish's or owl's
absorbing all sleepless nights, self-righteous yowls.

By the time they send me out, I've grown fat
with their poison. But I have two stomachs:
One takes venom in, the other turns it to chyme.

They thought they'd make me lonely—banished
to the wilderness, but here among the scrub
and weeds I find new friends. In fact

we've formed a little club. Past midnight
each in our separate cave we hear
each other croon outrageous sorrow, mournful lays

preferring our separate cells, the better to compose.

I sing in the wilderness—words, rants, fables
all my own. They seize me in the middle
of a downpour and I cry out to the crowds:

Come, give me all your pain, your guilt, your thorns.
Fling them on my back like acid.
Watch them turn my brilliant-colored coat, sharpen up my horns.
I can chomp on any food you throw me, however rancid.

Cast off your wants, your gnashing rage;
I'll chew and chew and spit it on the page.

FIRENZE DREAM

In the middle of Firenze
with nowhere to sleep
my Italian not working right
except for *afoso*, meaning suffocating
heat, at which everyone nods
as they're trying to find me a bed
near the Duomo, whose Baptistery
I can see in the distance

until I wonder, *What is this
really about?*
and say, *Fear ends*
then *Friends*
and think I have it: the dreamed
city marking the transit
from woe to company.

The next day
after the disturbance of yet
another dream, in different weather (a man,
the accompanying sex guilt) I knew:
Frenzy. Frenzy.

BLUE DUTCH TIN

What made me hold on
to the blue Dutch tin
that once had stored a simple
cache of chocolates

you practically swallowed whole?
What made the officer give me the box
after he broke through your door,
found you face down?

I took it home to open
having first changed my locks.
On its lid clipper ships sailed and sheep
herded down a snowy path;

how could I find what had shook your heart
and felled you. I flushed the rest away.
From the empty tin a braying goat
flew out and fastened beneath my chin:

your father spewing lies: I'd watched
you die, then fled, pretended
the door was chained against me.
No matter the cop saw I couldn't get in.

No matter he gave me the tin.
No matter your room became
a box of sweets you'd
Houdini'd yourself in.

Is that why I've jammed the tin
with beaded glass the shade
of your sea-eyes, and amber—
sap within your tree that no longer rises?

I lift them out, set them gleaming
round my neck, let other men
seize me. The goat begins to shrivel,
loses its voice, drops from my throat.

And here you are
still listening
inside the tin each time
I open it.

BROKEN CHAIR

Some Museum of Modern Art original, circular
seat with rounded wooden arms,

in the Bauhaus style, belonged
to his yekke bubbe.

All the springs exposed in the seat, its cottony entrails always spilling
out (a light cloth covered it) where his calico cat would sleep.

Why did he never have it reupholstered? Once he said
he would when his new life (did he mean ours?) began.

One night a chair-spring gashed open the cat's belly dripping blood.
At the all-night animal hospital the doctors stitched her closed.

He never fixed the chair. Seven years ago to the day, some old story uncoiled
inside, struck him dead. His mother fled back home with him, a newborn;

at her father's bar she met another man, remarried; together
they coiled up in his ears, *This man's your dad.* Inside

he always knew it wasn't true, though he was well into his twenties
before he found his father. Of course it's only in retrospect I see

the cat and the chair—twin witnesses—in the basement room where he OD'd:
the cat cowering under the bed, the wretched chair (so precious to him)

as his hold on something honest and broken and tied to him in blood.

If he had lived, we'd have wed, redone the chair. I might
be sitting in it now instead of piecing together

threads of a story
I can't repair

nor finish telling.

THE BAT

Barren of fear
save for the giddy bat

shadow flitting:

Is it the ghost of you
hitting the night walls?

I shout you out
into the dark hall of souls

ricocheting for the echo
of some body to seize and inhabit.

Or is this random fright
oscillating through the night halls

my refusal to call it over:
end the one-way conversation

with a fluttering pair of ears.

REAWAKENING

Now I understand the Christian mystery:
It's not that the beloved dies and ascends
to heaven, having been
horribly pierced,
but that he rises
fully impossibly whole.

As though the one I saw today
eating outdoors
really was the lost one
revived: the bruise on his forehead
where he'd hit the floor
fully healed.
And the price of his return is
he doesn't know who I am.

PAST THE ALLOWABLE LIMIT OF GRIEF

(letter to B.)

I know I am not forbidden to write to you anymore—
after nine years we have begun having commerce in dreams—
but I've no one else to speak to who knew you
not your mother, father, sister, cousins,
who threw me out of their yellow circle of grief
before the week of Shivah was out—even our betrothal
erased from their stories and your stone. See. I've got nothing
new to offer or tell. You know—if there is still a you to know—
that I've married, borne a son—isn't that called moving on?
Then why as the year rounds to autumn and I shake the lulav
and etrog am I always reminded of the first time I held the citron up
and wanted to offer it to you—though we had not spoken yet—
as though its spiced body were mine? Is it because we met
in the sukkah of bees and just two years later
it's almost biblical that practically the last thing you did
and certainly my last image of you—the frozen snapshot I carry—
you are standing in the street waving the Israeli flag—
you who hated all signs of the patriot? I still can't picture how
you could have died alone—at midnight—fighting for your heart
on the night of Torah scrolls being unrolled from the beginning—
on Sabbath eve no less—your body—dare I say it—
an unraveled scroll—naked—on the floor where they found you
the next day—where I sent them to find you.
I know your bones wear your tallis your mother found in a top
drawer in a moment of lucid movement after your body
had been lifted away and before grief came to cloak her in fire.
And I know it is not meet to grieve so long—that my life
has at last a stable fineness to it (even a room of my own)
and the words *I miss you* don't say it don't begin to conjure
with my sad anger at your last mistake—
the white powder you breathed to ratchet up your happiness—

or the way my going on moves me further away from you
but like a lighthouse: your pleasure at everything—even the wine
rilling down the glass's inside had *great legs*—I carry with me
to lighten my way.

III

OPENING THE SCROLL

For you, the tongue
    unscrolling its song
        down the body.

Nights I work best
    and you're more willing
        parchment

I wet and wet;
    conjoined with me, you
        add your own

lines inside the dance we make of us.
    Antiphony to mine:
        a child's wild squiggle

on a magic slate of wax—
    just lift the sheet,
        erase, relax and start again

while the world's sky rushes its
    stars overhead, passes on
        to that blue our elders used—

and we've lost—for coloring prayer
    shawl and fringe. I throw my head back
        each morning and it's there

above my face
    with its daylight
        wind.

I offer this thanksgiving:
    that the dark night
        should yield, transit us

into such a lighted wood where, unblinded,
    arising, our bodies sing
        the morning praise.

SPRING RITES

So he took us
       into the desert
once more

out of the constricted—
       into the stark
wave of bright fire

air whipping sand
       in our faces.
We got pulled into

the large ear of the sea
       then out onto a shore of loss
so that now we have nothing

but these palms
       heavy with coriander, honeyed prayers
raised to any rough wind

he would have us enter.

Who ever thought
       freedom could feel
like bricks

as we wander together

inside of days filled
       with such profuse cloudy light
no words come—just

this crepuscular sun
       with its moody shining—
then nights of stray windy fire

until we're awakened
      by a voice stuttering out
blessings

as though they were
      unscrolling
the concealed map.

CLIMBING MOUNT SINAI

The shock was all that ice
and my grey-bearded guide seeking
to dissuade me from
the ascent.

I scaled anyway, pointed
to my strong legs
though I slipped, could
grab no toe- or finger-
hold.

My persistence
made him
disappear.

Alone, as any Moses
would have to be,
I continued

To the summit to find a sea
beaten by winds
and a pool in the middle
into which I was supposed to dive.

Where were the tablets, I wondered.
Written on our bodies, the wind's swift reply.

Female and male
naked, side-to-side,
making a covenant
in rough water, on teeming land.

BELIEVERS IN MERCY

This is how Noah must have felt:
Go to sleep, rain. Wake up, rain.
The wooden flaps on the cabin leaking inside.

This is how the world often ends:

The animals getting restive—too busy huddling
in the cold wet wind to mate or eat.

No one thinks about the cries of the thousand
thousand creatures who floated on
branches, the leftover pieces of houses—

Those others who cursed Noah and his family,
suffocating on water, paddled off
into history's amnesia.

They were the best of carpenters, they the gatherers
of pomegranates now floating on the surface
of rivers, they the trappers of birds—whose wet feathers
made them too heavy to fly and an easy catch,
though no fire will take—they the believers in mercy.

Surely the rain will stop before everyone drowns
and the crops are all smothered. Before the grain
all rots in its storage sacks
carried to higher and ever higher ground.

Being descended from Noah, I should side with his story.

But there must have been some deserving
of forgiveness: women craving someone
else's man, petty gamblers,
avaricious husbands, envious children.

Outside, save for the chosen pair:
Field mice squeal all night in the rain,
raccoons knit their claws in prayer and finally live
peaceably together, the groundhog is rained out of his hole.

MY SOUL'S WARDROBE

> By all means use sometimes to be alone;
> Salute thyself; see what thy soul doth wear.
> —George Herbert, *The Church Porch*

Today I'll wear a cool summer coat
an anxious spray of blue-green needles
porcupine of the tall Scotch pine.

Later I'll wear a lake of slate-grey hope
shivery weather with lots of heather
loose foliage of late summer alpine.

By late morning I'll sport a scarf of wind at my throat
not too lazy, very hazy, impatient weather
of wanting to swim in this woodsy pond by wild lupine.

Or else by midday I'll doff a cap and row a boat
out to the shimmery island of black walnut trees
and wild blueberries where goldenrod wave in a line.

By afternoon I'll don my cape of white oak
and go find a pure oak stand where I'll sit
as still as a tree or a bird or a vine of spicy woodbine.

OSGOOD POND

Lake water held
    the last bit of light
late into twilight

last night sky caught
    on the lower rims of clouds
eggplant or kidney bean

selvage of light
    we gaped until it
vanished

while morning sunlight
    is so clear it casts
        green shadows on paper
birch trunks sketches

a stand of pines on the lake's surface
    upon which the trees
        not easily outdone throw down
a copy of themselves in paler green

so some passing fancy can muse
    about fish that do indeed
        at least at bright midday
harbor themselves in trees.

OLIVETTA

Little no-name beach
I return to
four years later
with you
has a name
and water as blue
as the finest
ultramarine of the painters
of the *cinquecento*
(that's where it all gathers
and remains)
as in the sky
to lose myself
if not for you who waits
at the shore reading—
Panama hat on head:
my personal steeple
my true north
my great fish of the air.

KRUPP'S WALK

On Capri, we're all understudies for beauty.

Even the grapevines, trellised purple horns of morning glories
    overhead bushes of oleander and bougainvillea
olive trees, pines, cypresses that gather up afternoon
    heat and release it as light.

Even those who adorn their dark bodies with coral and gold:
    the blonde who waxes his face in the mirror, the fat lady
in the shade who shares sandwiches with her terrier, the woman
    who appears to be talking madly to no one or the sea
who sits with her back to her husband who stands stretching his dark
    hairy chest against her and the sun and says nothing, simply nothing.

Even the old man reading a paper all day who reserves a lounge chair
    for his book as though he were waiting for someone
and the American woman half in tree-shade who sometimes uses the page
    for a mirror, who swam out among the fish until her dream
of being a fish passed, and now leaves her hair in a salty braid
    for the long climb home.

THE NATURALIST DECLARES HER IGNORANCE

Now that I've learned to identify three trees
by name, that still leaves

many unnameable with leaves ovoid
or crescent-shaped, bark rough, scratchy
grey, or smooth brown

and all those wildflowers along the road:
lavender thistles, red-berried or orange-
tongued, or full of pale blue sprays.

I've flown over the ocean to admire flowers
anonymously trailing in vines on road-
sides and ogled fish feeding in schools

or singly burrowing in underwater caves

and craned my head for birds diving into
the lake's fragrant mirror
and have barely been able to name one.

Even the tree I'm sitting beside: ridgy oval-leafed
at water's edge—not a fir, not a pine, definitely not a
eucalyptus—could be I'll never learn its proper name.

A fellow poet rebuked me once for not knowing
that was joe-pye weed all along the roadside
as though a poet should call things by their proper names.

I'd like to think that poems like the vast expanse of lake must lie
unnamed, when from the far end
the white-ringed loon gives his falsetto cry.

And though I'm thankful I know its name, I'd rather
resemble the speechless hill of trees
above the changing palette of the lake.

IV

STROKE

These days being so fuzzy-headed I go
into the Greek diner on 72nd Street the scaffolding

up all winter finally gone so the late spring light
streams through & I sit in the corner booth & order the usual

dark-meat turkey on rye which is almost a poem & a soda
when she limps in with one metal arm brace says hi to everyone

& me sits down at the next booth on the other side
two men are striking a deal about something in film

only her left arm works so it takes a while to slip everything
off & slide into the seat with her big belly a silver caduceus

flopping over her breasts she says hi to me a second time I'm watching
her closely since we share a not-so-secret sisterhood of the belly

though I'm a fairly new member I get up the nerve to ask
how many months & she struggles gesturing blurts I've-Had-a-Stroke

writes 6 over and over on the Formica with her left forefinger
until I nod then point to my belly hold up 4 fingers Nice-Beautiful

& we go on talking in gestures & simple retorts Makes-Sense-
Yes the waitress holds the menu up so she must be a regular

here & writes out TOAST so she can nod then tells me
IVF... Once-Nothing-Twice-Nothing-By-Myself-Beautiful

then points to me IVF-Once-Nothing-By-Myself-Chinese-Herbs
& she Yes! Makes-Sense! How old is she—38. How old am I—41.

Nice-Great-Makes-Sense-So-Worried when I ask about the stroke
she holds up 7 fingers for years. Have you tried . . . Everything she

waves it all away points to my small belly—Beautiful—now it's almost time
to go what can I give her I hold open a gallery catalogue bright swanks of color

You? No I write POET—Understand—She? After-No-Before Invest... Investment
Banker? Yes—Her name? Broo-Broomah... can't say it when the waitress returns

says Bluma And Yours? Sharon Nice-Makes-Sense

THE SEAGULL

The clipper ship in the bottle
the goose in the goose-neck bottle
the baby floating head down batlike in my belly
the seagull caged beneath the garbage pail
as I stand on upper Broadway peering through
the crowds at the bus stop peering through the mesh
at the seagull.

Larger than the random beach scavenger
tall as a two-year-old and broader—
his feathers are filthy—he stands nonplussed
in his makeshift metal cage in front of the bank.
Not a peep out of him while all the human
crows flock and descend: even seven policemen
from at least three different vehicles—one with

a box to transport him to a vet or humane
society—and a fire crew. He can't fly
and somehow landed on Broadway was hopping
all over the streets, the traffic island
until two brave women caught him
now themselves on video recounting
how they captured him beneath the steel pail where

he gazes out into all the meanings we make
of him, some of us wondering how
a seagull got on Broadway, forgetting
the ocean a few miles south the Hudson
two blocks west. The anomaly of things
caught inside things or thoughts:
how a soul gets caught in a body

and if it's true as the Greeks said:
The body is the candle wax, the soul
gives it shape; we burn it up until neither

remains. But how does the shape arise
how will this bump in my side emerge in
days as a foot attached to a body
which has a soul and what fire

will light it on its way so my passageway the
size of a thick finger will open and let a head
then a shoulder then another pass through? How
does the night open and the milky streaks
of light pour through—the fist of sleep loosened
so consciousness lying on its pillow wakens and
stretches into restlessness?

The seagull left upper Broadway in a police truck;
most of the spectators left on the buses
that stopped one by one. Things inside of things,
even the dead flickering in the heart (How do
we put them there how do they get there?)
and with a name called out in the dark they
break free of rib and muscle and fly they
soar they remain inside the cage of memory

fly back willingly.
But the clipper ship the goose the baby the seagull

AUBADE

Dawn cries, pries you awake. I lift you
onto your pillow & let you roll in
toward me & open your mouth—is there any
caress like this? Nothing like these two
small hands globing the breast I offer.
Coleridge's definition of the sublime: no similitude
possible. This is not *like* carnal love
or passion; it is what it is: itself.
Spring light & birdsong filtering through the
striped curtains, your gaze drinking in mine
as you hum & suck, I stroke the downy head
you rest in the crook of my arm. This is
our forever better than any other
sleep we fall back into.

ON READING AMICHAI'S *OPEN CLOSED OPEN*
WHILE SUCKLING SAMUEL

1.
Open the book above his head and drink in
stones, lovers of roasted almonds and tea mixing
what opens at death with what closes at birth.

Here I am conduit, completed circuit as children
learn of electrical current: left nipple tugged
open so milk sprays on a ready tongue,

right eye imbibing words of cinnamon milk
through an invisible straw. A tickling hand gropes,
closes, so filled to overflowing: *This* is the land

of milk & honey—our bodies, this endless book—
it makes him doze while I dip into verse
the way a biscuit, when dipped in milk, softens & sweetens & opens.

2.
Hannah got to keep Samuel until he was weaned.
Cease to wonder how long it took: as long
as possible—perhaps until he lost his milk

teeth—before she gave him up to serve
in God's house as she had vowed. Every mother
when she weans her son gives him up

to serve, if not God, then cup & plate,
if not plate & cup, then sky & birds,
if not birds & sky, then wagon & truck,
if not truck & wagon, then hands & faces,
if not faces & hands then full phrases

that open close open into the pages
he will turn for the rest of his nights & days.

THE SHADOW

At first an enlarging dark cloud
    like God's dark face moving through water
        a group of bathers
not unlike Israelites in the desert intently follows.

        On closer view it has angles
    shifts direction in a movement
too swift for the wind.

From the sign at the shore
    (STINGRAY SPAWNING
    —KINDLY SHUFFLE YOUR FEET)
        we jigsaw together
this dark fluxing mass in the shallows

though I had feared them invisible
underfoot as sand dollars or flounder

instead of this fleet school
    of flat birds flapping
        through ocean and our wonderment
close to the surface—and with tails!

        changing formation as we watch
    in the distance as I lift an arm
to signal *Here!* the baby is being hoisted

in mock flight by his dad
inside the cabana's hot shade.

MUSING ON A BRUISE

When the chair just crashed
    and we fell down back

on the straw trash I gripped him to me
    like life and took the blow to my rear.

So what's a mother to do
    when the baby wants to be

in her arms always even when
    she's at her desk in prayer

kneeling when she writes petitioning
    the air for words. Poems

are prayers after all
    overheard as Dante knew we're

merely scribes *ego scriptor*
    Pound wrote too. For weeks

after undressing I'd glance
    back at the mirror, perusing

my purple cheek a bruise
    I'd suffered for baby & poetry.

Now the chair's been fixed, the baby's
    outside on the slide

I'm back inside kneeling to hear.

HANDS

She had to have been years younger than I am now
    my mother
though her 42 will always be older than
    my 42
when I'd study the backs of her hands particularly her
    right hand
with its raised river of blue blood coursing just below
    the surface
and I'd push down on those strong veins and marvel:
    Would I ever
achieve such a thing? Those the days when television's
    blue light
reigned over all our intimacies on the bed in talks later on
    in games
of Scrabble, when you learned from a commercial
    the roughness
of a woman's hands belied her age.

Now that the baby is beginning to play with the backs of
    my hands
(though as a boy he'll surely want to emulate
    me less)
though my hands have never grown as large as hers (how
    could they?)
raised rivers thinner lower more
    a tracery
of blue-grey streams beneath the surface
    I'm reminded
that what I hated most back then were her
    palms after
she'd broken down been taken away to be
    shocked
force-fed pills then brought back home
    somnambulant
all I'd need do was look at her hands thumbs

lying spatulate
inside her palms—useless—to know the waters
        had risen
till *she* was barely she.

It's always been the way I've measured someone—
        strangers on the subway
lovers and friends—what are their hands like?
        Don't we all
do that—find some part or quality
        to fix
on and apprize? Sometimes now in sleep my left thumb
        strays mid-palm
for comfort. Years ago I would have wrenched it free
        for fear
it was a sign my mind was letting go. Now I
        let it
seek succour where it may even in shadowy
        similitude.

COME BACK

I know you've come back: a six-year-old
    playing on the monkey bars

in the park where your grandson
    crawls around & looking up

he might, as babies do, recognize
    you—his face in your face

as I have seen yours in his.
    It's strange this metempsychosis:

In three weeks you shed your life;
    eleven months after the soul gyred

free of personality coils
    itself inside the fetal sac.

I know you're back, I sense it
    when my son's grin turns scowl

at some too-sour fruit or in
    calm reflection on the motion

of pigeons, pages of a book,
    his face assumes your serious look.

It's him, it's you, you're somewhere settling in-
    to your evening bath he's splashing in.

PSALM

Where did I hear God can't read
so that's why all prayers must be recited
aloud sung *abundant praises for the chief*
musician who can't read a note tonight
is Yom Kippur and I have nothing to atone for
but my lack of gratitude (oh sure some residual
anger impatience gossip lust) abundant
praises for the chief musician who allowed
life to pour from my life a small
downy head to nestle at my breast
(even God can't suckle!) but I
give thanks (not like the alligators whose young
snap and practically kill at birth) let
Samuel whose name means *my prayer was heard*
continue to thrive on my sweet milk
for as long as he wishes and let all the unknowns
of my life unroll in their time as does this praise
because God doesn't turn pages he leaves
that to young babies who scroll from their
mother's bodies to sing in a language
even God knows.

THE WHITE LINE

I was crawling along the floor painting a white
    line with my body
as I'd go sometimes feeling rebellious I'd make it zig-
    zag: a bunch
of knotty squiggles so it was barely a line
    at all then go back
to crawling so the line grew straight as a divider
    on the highway
the baby right behind me forging his own
    steady white line
out of his body though more slowly so sometimes
    he'd fall behind
have to catch up rounding the corner after
    losing sight of
me for a moment we continued this way until
    I could see
I'd been travelling a square circuit—or at least a series
    of straight moves
with turns that in one more span would bring me back
    to the start—
when he woke me with his morning cry and I stopped crawling
    rose to find him
at the door we were sitting together in the dawn light
    he was drawing
the line of milk out of me hazily I saw
    this line
(Would it have been better if I'd been able to
    complete it—)
as my life (—or was *he* completing it competing it opening
    it up-
ending it open-ending it

NOTES

"The Realm of the Possible": The epigraph is from Cees Nooteboom's novel *Rituals*, translated by Adrienne Dixon (Louisiana State University Press, 1983). The definition of love is taken from Aristophanes's famous speech in Plato's *The Symposium* (translated by Walter Hamilton). The story of Salvia is drawn from Ettore Settani's *Miti Uomini e Donne di Capri*. This poem is for Barry.

"Uncanny": The first stanza retells and quotes from the story, "Two Dogs Under a Rock," from John Berger's *Photocopies* (Pantheon Books, 1996).

"Betrayal": "Sei cattivo" means "You're being naughty" in Italian.

"Roman Punch": "Porta fortuna" means "It's lucky" in Italian.

"Geniza": Geniza refers to the respectful burial or storage of torn or damaged Hebrew texts containing God's name. Some genizas also include the records of the Jewish community. The world's largest geniza has been discovered in Cairo—part of the upper story of the Ben Esra synagogue—whose texts scholars deem as important as the Dead Sea Scrolls.

"On the Unmiraculous": The story of the Prophet Elisha and the Shunammite woman appears in *Kings*, Book II, verses 8-37.

"Broken Chair": "Yekke bubbe" means "German-Jewish grandmother" in Yiddish.

"Past the Allowable Limit of Grief": On the holiday of Sukkot, the Festival of Booths, Jews traditionally shake a *lulav*: a cluster of myrtle, willow, and palm branches, as well as an *etrog*: a citron. The Sukkah (booth) is the temporary dwelling the Israelites set up while wandering in the desert.

A NOTE ABOUT THE AUTHOR

Sharon Dolin is the author of two previous books of poems, *Heart Work* (The Sheep Meadow Press) and *Serious Pink* (Marsh Hawk Press), and four chapbooks: *The Seagull* (The Center for Book Arts), *Mistakes* (Poetry New York Pamphlet Series), *Climbing Mount Sinai* (Dim Gray Bar Press), and *Mind Lag* (Turtle Watch Press). She has been the recipient of a Fulbright Scholarship to Italy and a national award from the Poetry Society of America, and she has held several fellowships to the Virginia Center for the Creative Arts and Yaddo. She is the coordinator and co-judge of the Center for Book Arts Annual Letterpress Poetry Chapbook Competition and a curator of the Center Broadsides Reading Series. She has taught at The Cooper Union, The New School, and New York University. She currently teaches poetry seminars and workshops at the Unterberg Poetry Center of the 92nd Street Y and lives in New York City with her husband and son.